Animal Reincarnation
Everything You Always Wanted to Know!

BRENT ATWATER
Just Plain Love® *Books*

Copyright information © 2000-2011 by B. Brent Atwater
Published and Distributed in the United States by: Brent Atwater's
Just Plain Love® Books
www.BrentAtwater.com or www.JustPlainLoveBooks.com

Editorial: Brent Atwater	Cover Design: Brent Atwater
Interior Design: Brent Atwater	Illustrations: Brent Atwater

All rights reserved. No part of this book may be reproduced by any mechanical, photographic or electronic process or in the form of a phonographic reading: nor may it be stored in a retrieval system transmitted, or otherwise
be copied for public or private use- other than for "fair use" as brief quotations embodied in articles and reviews without prior written permission of the publisher and author.

The author of this book, Brent Atwater, is not a medical doctor nor associated with any branch of allopathic medicine. Brent is an Integrative Holistic Energy Medicine specialist in Medical Intuitive Diagnosis.
Brent offers her opinions based on her intuition. ALWAYS consult a physician or trained health care professional either directly or indirectly concerning any physical or medical problem or condition before undertaking any diet, health related technique or lifestyle change program.

The contents presented herein are derived from the author's intuition and experiences and not intended as substitutes for treatment by a physician or other healthcare professionals. The intent of the author is only to offer information of a general nature to help facilitate your journey to health and well-being. In the event you choose to use any of the information in this book for yourself, which is your constitutional right, as in traditional medicine, there are no guarantees, and the author and the publisher assume no responsibility for your actions.

Library of Congress Cataloging-in-Publication Data

Paperback ISBN: 1456439502
EAN-139781456439507
Hardcover ISBN:
EBook ISBN:
Kindle: ASIN: B004GUSB6A
Audio:

1st printing: 2011 USA
Canada
UK, AU, SA check with distributor
Publisher's Price Higher in Other Countries
Animals/Pet / Lifestyles / Self-Help / Spiritual Growth / Inspirational / Pet Loss/ Pet Grief Support / Body, Mind & Spirit / Reincarnation / Spirituality / Family & Relationships / Death / Grief / Bereavement / Self Development / Healing / Nonfiction / Animals / Pets/ Pets / Cats / General/ Cats / Pets / Animal Stories/ Pet Heaven/ Audio Books / eBooks

Visit Brent Atwater's Web sites at:
www.BrentAtwater.com
www.JustPlainLoveBooks.com

This *Just Plain Love*® Book
is given to

To: _____

Message: _____

_____

Date: _____

with
LOTS of LOVE, HUGS and KISSES!!!

From: _____

Acknowledgements

I want to thank you the reader
for taking the time to explore my
Just Plain Love® Books
and for allowing me to share what I have learned
and am learning about pet past lives,
animal reincarnation and animal communication
through my and other individuals personal
experiences.

Special thanks to Michael Wellford
and my precious fur, finned and feathered
companions for their contributions and enduring
patience with me and my spiritual path.

It is my intent and hope
that this information will facilitate
inspiration, greater perspectives and
expanded awareness in your life.

I thank those who have supported and encouraged
my journey
and the authors, speakers and teachers
who contributed to shaping my consciousness.

My gratitude also goes to:
Each individual who has shared their story with me
in order for readers to derive hope and be inspired by
"all that is."

A special thank you to
Lisbeth and her cat Merlin
whose bond represents
why I write
my animal and pet reincarnation books.

Dedication

This is written to honor my entire inspiring and
beloved canine, feline, equine and other animal
teachers, guardians and companions
(including "Fishy") with whom I shared
my experiences, learning and life.
From my heart to yours, thank you!

My special love goes to each and every one of you
for filling my heart with joy.

To Thomas Michael Ramseur Wellford,
whose life, love, and passing
made my understanding possible.
I shall always hold you
and hear you in my heart,
my soul, and my dreams.

To those very special people and fur babies
who are my joy,
and with whom I share
hope, laughter and LIFE!!!

TABLE OF CONTENTS

Personalized Message & Gift Page	v
Acknowledgments	vii
Dedication	viii
Table of Contents	ix
Introduction	xi
Reincarnation	17
History	21
Physical Death	23
The Transition Process	23
Grief	24
Affirmation to Assist in Transition	25
Signs the Transition Process Has Begun	26
Prayers for Reincarnation	27
Prayer for Signs That Your Pet will Reincarnate	28
Prayer to Assist Your Pet in Reincarnating	28
Can I Talk My Pet Into Coming Back?	29
How Many Times Can An Animal Reincarnate?	30
God Animals	33
Can a Pet Return as a Human?	36
Animals that Behave like Humans	
What is an "Over Soul"?	
Can My Animal Reincarnate into Another Pet Form?	38
Can the Animal Born Before My Pet Died, be My Pet?	40
What is a "Walk In?"	
What is a "Soul Braid?"	

How Long Does Reincarnation Take?	43
Communicating With Your Pet on the Other Side	44
What Can Affect the Communication with My Pet	44
Signs Your Pet is Contacting You from the Other Side	45
How to Contact Your Pet's Energy & Bring It to Earth	49
How to Find & Touch Your Deceased Pet's Energy	50
Is Contacting My Pet's Energy Selfish?	53
What can Prohibit My Pet from Visiting Me?	54
The Signs and Stages of Your Pet's Reincarnation Grieving	55
Reconnection: How Will We Get Back Together?	58
Recognition: How Will I Recognize My Pet?	60
Confirmation	63
Reuniting: "I'm Home!"	65
Questions From The Audience	68
About the Author	75
The *Just Plain Love*® Story	79
Join Our Groups & Follow Friend	83
Other *Just Plain Love*® Titles	85

INTRODUCTION

If you are reading this introduction you're probably an animal lover or someone you know needs a GREAT BIG HUG!

If you just plain love® animals or have experienced the loss of a beloved furry, feathered or finned soul mate, have an interest in pet past lives, animal reincarnation, animal communication or care about another individual who is grieving over the loss of their much loved animal companion, this is THE animal reincarnation book for you!

The Animal Reincarnation Guide answers almost every question that you can think of about the pet and animal reincarnation process. It teaches you how to ask your pet if they are going to reincarnate, ways to find and recognize them on the other side and techniques on how to touch your animal's energy on the other side.

Brent Atwater's full color companion books - "I'm Home!" a Never Ending Love Story trilogy about Dogs, Cats and Horses shares love filled heartwarming stories that illustrate the various signs and different events that led owners to be reunited with their beloved reincarnated animal companions.

Ms Atwater offers her dog Friend's past lives and multiple reincarnation in her lifetime as the foundation of all "I know from my heart and soul's experiences during each of my beloved pets' sickness, degenerating health, disease, chronic illness and even sudden or inevitable death to crossing over the Rainbow Bridge.

Many thanks to all God's wonderful and cherished creatures who have taught me what I share with you in this book that I write to honor all their lives."

This book derives its research information from the multitude of international interspecies stories gathered over the years.

Each animal reincarnation is the embodiment of the lessons each owner learned and how their heart's awareness evolved with each death and rebirth, and how each guardian's mind expanded with new found realities from that animal's past life and new incarnation.

"Reliving each story inside my heart while checking the formatting, spelling and editing this book was difficult. I hope my research will give strength to your heart and support what you are going though or seeking to learn.

It is my intent that this book comforts your heart, reassures and helps inspire your hope, in addition to providing insight that expands your awareness of all things possible and real! I expect these true stories give you tingles and goose bumps (a friend calls them God bumps) of confirmation, and that you can relate to the thoughts, feeling and experiences of each owner and perhaps think
                Hummmmmm,
that relates to what's going on in my life!

As a holistic integrative energy medicine specialist, throughout the decades as a medical intuitive, I've gathered the results, stories and testimonials from clients, friends and family members, (in addition to my personal experiences), that concluded we all experienced profound healing and expanded awareness when we recognized that our beloved animal companions reincarnated to be with us again.

Enjoy!

For future books
Please submit your animal's reincarnation story to:

Brent@BrentAtwater.com
BrentAtwater@live.com

My reincarnation research began over 15 years ago when I lost my fiancé in an unexpected auto accident. I wanted to find him! I started researching ways that his energy could return to me.

While studying this process, I became more and more aware that my dogs were similar and demonstrated extremely if not downright exact character traits of each other.

When "Friend" my border collie was born with a "B" on his bottom that exactly matched my signature, I took that as my sign to write about the expanded awareness my soul understood and that my heart had come to know to be true.

Furthering my research and documenting the evidence I was collecting, I gathered true stories from around the globe, each teaching me more about reincarnation and the animal kingdom. I wanted stories about live pets that had reincarnated multiple times within each owner's life, like Friend had done in mine, and other stories that validated and illustrated an example of each nuance of my research.

I wanted the reader to be able to touch those real animals and be able to talk to their guardians to hear "their story," so no one could say I "made this stuff up!"

This book represents the insights from gleaning through mounds of similar evidence within each story, and from all of the various questions asked on TV and radio shows, in the various workshops, lectures, presentations and book signings that I have done and will do.

Whenever I think that I have covered E-V-E-R-Y question, another one comes along and I revise this Animal Reincarnation Guide about every 6 months to reflect my latest and most current knowledge base of questions and answers.

It is my intent to educate readers by inspiring expansion of their awareness through opening their minds to the thought that animal reincarnation is a very real possibility, and for those "knowing through personal experience," a confirmed and definite reality!

The Animal Reincarnation Guide:
<u>Everything You Always Wanted to Know!</u>

When you've lost your beloved pet, service animal, companion animal, assistance dog, therapy pet, soul pet partner and forever finned, feathered or fur baby, - "love of your life," your "heart and soul and everything good in the world" "child," don't lose hope. Listen to your heart's urgings, watch your dreams, and follow your soul's knowing. Pay attention to your intuition and inner guidance.

If you feel that you want to or must hold onto your pet's beds, belongings and toys, there is a reason. Some part of your soul's inner being knows that they will be back.

Each and every animal's soul is a spirit composed of eternal energy that lives forever in our vast Universe. Whether or not it's your soul pet, forever fur baby, animal spirit guide or spiritual teacher in an animal form, God/ the Universe honors his choice to reincarnate in whatever way to be with you in various physical bodies throughout your life time.

It's not **just** about your animal's soul's path or singular lessons, your pet's reincarnation, "walk in," "over soul" or "soul braid" is about what you have to accomplish **together**.

He/she will continue to reincarnate, "walk in," "soul braid" or "over soul" until your combined learning opportunities are complete.

It's about the human animal spiritual soul arrangement that you each have made to one another.

Know that your pet is never gone forever. He's just changed the form of his life force energy.

Give your animal's energy and spirit time to recover, recalibrate, regenerate, choose or relocate in a new body if they choose to return.

Your heart will know when it's time to look for them again.

When you reunite with them, your souls will instantly recognize each other since you have already blended and are familiar with each other's energy earlier in this lifetime.

Your spirit will resonate with and feel their energy's return to say "*I'm Home!*"

History:

The belief in Reincarnation dates back as far as the ancient Egyptians in addition to the Buddhist and Hindu religions, Jainism and Taoism. Simply put, to believe in reincarnation means you believe that the soul's life force energy is immortal i.e. ongoing and infinite.

Animal reincarnation is sometimes called transmigration; a process that the Hindu religion and others believe happens after someone dies. This process is about the belief that the spirit of the deceased person moves into the body of another person or animal. The Yogic view also embraces the transmigration process.

Regular reincarnation belief is that when one's physical body dies their spirit is able to choose to be reborn into another body because the energy known as the spirit or soul is everlasting. It's usually a belief that the body that the soul chooses is based on its past life Karma and its karmic purpose with you. Therefore to me, it is a reasonable expectation that many people would believe their pets will reincarnate.

Although not all people believe in reincarnation; it's interesting that most people agree that you will be with all your pets that have gone to the Rainbow Bridge when your body dies and crosses to the other side.

FYI, in 2007 a respected British leading independent research company YouGov conducted a study and found that dogs proved to be the type of animal most likely to be considered a reincarnation by pet owners: 51% said they had or have dogs in which they believe to be a re-incarnation while 44% said it was a cat.

Some individuals, who have not experienced the real life opportunity and true knowing of a reincarnated pet, feel that pets do not return because they have no need to or that the animals don't have lessons to learn.

Others who have not experienced an angel animal that reincarnates suggest that a loved one who passed may have sent you a special furry, finned or feathered baby to be with you. In my experience, animals reincarnate for diverse reasons.

A soul connected forever pet is usually a spiritual teacher, guide or guardian spirit that travels with you in pet form throughout your earthly journey.

The reincarnation information herein was researched and gathered from friends, clients and my personal experiences. We all believe that in my dog Friend's and each of our individual's pet's life reality and in whatever form they choose, animals DO reincarnate!

Use any information that resonates with you and remember-

There can always be exceptions!

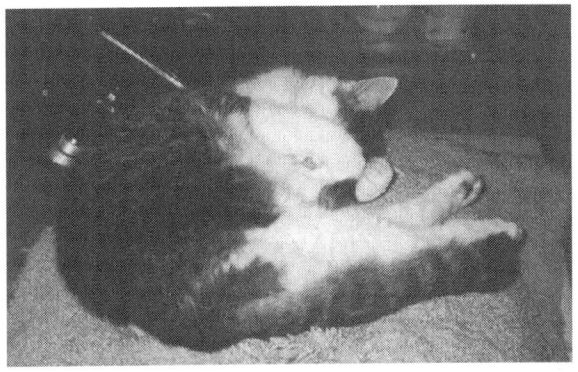

Physical Death is the Beginning:

Each physical body provides an opportunity to depart, whether it ages, is physically broken or ill, just wears out or just opts out in a birth or newborn process. It's part of the trading spaces process. Due to shorter life spans, upgrading to a healthier body is a necessity for our beloved animals, birds, fish or reptiles so they can continue sharing your life's journey.

If you are reading this book prior to the impending passage of the love of your life, KNOW that death and transition is the **first** step in reuniting with you. This fact will help you during the transition and waiting process.

The Transition Process:

During the transition process, your pet's physical body will be in conflict with its soul's love for you and wanting to stay with you in your current situation.

Oftentimes when a pet is preparing to pass, and you are asking them to "hang on" for your sake:
> The pet will walk away from you
> Not look at you in your eyes
> Avoid their normal personal contact habits with you
> Stay or hide in another room trying to avoid your conflicting energy.

Another sign of impending transition is when you see an older or sickly pet sitting at a window or door staring out as if they are memorizing their last earthly view. They are!

Is it important to believe in reincarnation?
Yes. Your open minded energy facilitates the return of your pet more readily. Negative energy creates a barrier.

If you do not completely believe in reincarnation and might entertain the concept, hold the thought that "at least I'll give it a try, Why not?" Then your pet can come back more easily if it has chosen to do so.

Grief:
Since your beloved companion is so connected to you, your crying depletes your pet's energy and hampers their ability to transition in the best way possible!

Give your "baby" permission to do **as they so choose**. Honor their journey so they can be a part of yours quicker! It's all about mutual love and respect, although this is so hard to do in critical times.

Focusing your attention and emotions on their DEATH will slow down the reincarnation re-entry process!

Affirmation to assist your pet's transition:

The affirmation below will assist your cherished companion in transitioning easier and without horrific physical complications.

1. Hold its front paws with your hands or place the hand that you write with (that's your energy sending hand) on the pet's body near its heart.

2. Look into your pet's eyes if possible but not necessary. Ask with your heart or voice out loud: (This can be said one time or as often as you wish.)

"Fill in blank with Pet's name, I love you.
I honor, respect and support your choices.
From the love in my heart, I send you my life force energy to use as you so choose."

Your intent with this specific declaration will assist in making your pet's transition as gentle as possible. Do not change the wording or it will change the type of energy being sent.

It is imperative that you use the words **"as you so choose"** so your pet can use that additional energy boost provided from the love of your heart to either cross over or to get better--- Then it's THEIR choice!

Usually after you have said this phrase, at some point in time before they cross the Rainbow Bridge, your pet will create a tender *memory moment* as their way of acknowledging your love and releasing them to complete this incarnation's soul's path.

A client's cat was extremely ill for months and stayed alone in her bed in a dark corner. Several days after the client started saying the affirmation above, her cat got up, came over to sit in her lap and purred for the first time since her illness began. Later that night she calmly went to sleep (unassisted) in the safe haven of her owner's love while her guardian was stating this affirmation.

Signs the Transition Process is Imminent:

Before or during the timeframe when your pet starts withdrawing its life force energy, which is usually 24 – 48 hours prior to leaving its body. You can see its aura gradually diminish. During that time or beforehand you can ask your pet if it is going to reincarnate.

If you do not see auras, as an animal's electromagnetic life force energy becomes more centrally organized near the heart area, the animal's physical body becomes colder throughout their entire system as their energy is being incrementally withdrawn in preparing to depart. This progressive physical process starts as cold paws and ears, then lackluster or nonresponsive eyes, etc.

Prayers for Reincarnation:
When you want to ask your pet if it's going to reincarnate,
hold your pet's front paws with your hands or place your hand on the pet's body near its heart, look into its eyes if possible and ask with your heart or out loud:

I ask and it is my intent to know if we will be together again in this lifetime.
Will you return to live with me again in this lifetime?"

Your heart will hear the answer.
If you do not receive an answer, it may be due to the fact that your pet has not made their decision yet.
If you do not receive an answer that you feel is clear and factual due to the emotional upheaval that everyone is experiencing, then use the prayers set forth in a later section, to receive a response after your pet is on the other side.

I can tell if a pet is going to reincarnate by the fact that as a medical intuitive I can see inside an animal's current body and their future physical energy body. I am able to determine if and when an animal is going to reincarnate.

Although physical death may and does seem so very heart wrenching and permanent, you *must remember* that it is the FIRST step toward reincarnation. They need to shed that old body for a newer better version!

Prayer for Confirmation Signs:
I ask and it is my intent to know if _DASH GOLDMAN_ is going to return to be with me in this lifetime.

Please give me 3 signs within the next three days that I can easily understand that allows me to know in my heart whether or not my beloved pet is coming back to me in this lifetime. Thank you.

Prayer to Assist Your Pet in Reincarnating:
I ask and it is my intent to send _DASH_ (the deceased pet's name) from the love in my heart, my life force energy to use as you so choose. So be it, it is done.

The love in your heart transcends all realms. If your pet is going to choose to reincarnate, using this prayer after they have crossed will provide the extra energy boost to help them realign for reincarnation and help them transition back to earth more easily.

The key is to state these exact words: **"to use as you so choose."** Then your pet will determine the perfect timing for their healthy return.

Can I talk my pet into coming back?

I know a lady that wanted her "four legged fur baby" back so badly and quickly that when her pet complied with her wishes and reincarnated. It was in less than perfect physical health and form.

The results from rushing the reincarnation process "perfect timing" can be less than desirable. Again, be sure to state "to use as you so choose." Be patient for "perfect timing" in order for your pet to make the most appropriate and healthiest reentry.

To honor your pet, know it's **their** soul's choice. The spiritual agreement made between each of you was contracted before each of you entered this incarnation. To request to revise your previous agreement could promote unhealthy Karma.

I wrote a pet loss gift book about my reincarnated dog Friend, *"the Dog with a "B" on His Bottom,"* to prove that your prayers will be answered in perfect timing! "B"elieve and "B" inspired to hold onto your hope.
Don't rush timing!

How many times can an animal reincarnate?

- Each pet has its individual soul's path as you do.

Sometimes a pet will only be with you one time in your entire life. That single incarnation is their "path" and contract with you. You will know within your heart if your pet is returning.

You will also know if he isn't reincarnating. Your strong human animal soul bond, intuition and prior soul arrangements and spiritual agreements creates this "knowing."

If a pet is on earth just to learn their own lesson, it will usually only inhabit one incarnation.

Sometimes your pet will reincarnate many times WITH you, and learn their lessons while sharing the experience with you.

Friend with the "B" on his bottom got stolen from my locked car, escaped during rush hour traffic and was hit. He suffered broken ribs, bleeding lungs, shifted intestines, and a horrific black tire tread mark implanted in his beautiful white ruff. Medically, he should not be alive today. It was his lesson to think and "B" more discerning with his hugs to strangers while spreading the word about reincarnation.

- **An animal can choose multiple reincarnations** within their human companion's current lifespan or multiple lifetimes. The more learning and teaching you have to experience together (key word), the more often your pet will reincarnate to evolve with you during each of your incarnations.

- **A pet that is an old soul** and has been here many times and has completed his path with you does not have to return.

It's that pet's choice to reincarnate again if he wants to accompany you on your life's journey. A lot of "old soul" pets will lead you to and be the "over soul" i.e. the guiding essence, for a new replacement, rather than personally return.

- **Sometimes a baby, adolescent or young animal** that has unexplained or sudden onset medical problems or lots of medical conditions will choose to depart earth early in life.

Their souls are getting rid of the "sick" body in order to exchange it for a healthier one. Upon the reincarnate's reentry, their new more durable fur, finned or feathered form can live longer to share a more extended lifetime with you.

"Finding Gunner" in *"I'm Home!" a Cat's Never Ending Love Story* will warm your heart about a kitten who kept trying!!

- **We have seen on numerous occasions, animals that reincarnate only to stay until their owner passed over.**

One touching story was about a stray kitten that just "showed up!" It came to sit in her owner's lap while she was wheelchair bound during the end stage diseases of her life. When the owner passed, within 3 days, that perfectly healthy cat died in her sleep to join her owner.

- **Sometimes an animal will reincarnate to mirror the medical condition or take on the same health issues of its owner.**

The animal's medical plight will often help their owner learn more about treating their disorder.

God Animals are special old souls, all knowing animals that usually come for a major specific purpose or event. An example would be the bomb sniffing dog that was killed while saving a platoon of servicemen and women, or a dog that retrieved a child from drowning in a pool, or a cat that saved its family from a fire. A God Animal usually has one heroic task to complete on earth for and with their person or family or in service to humanity.

A God Animal can also be the emotional educational catalyst for the rest of your life, or teach its owner the most important Karmic lesson their guardian needs to learn.

If the owner does not "get" the lesson the animal was supposed to teach, that pet will reincarnate again and go through the entire process, until their owner understands and changes the behavior that needed modification.

At that point of newfound wisdom, the animal may choose at its discretion to return or it may have "signed on" for even more learning opportunities!

An example: A puppy ran out into the road and was killed. The owner learned to NEVER allow pets near a road. After that the pet chose to return to share happy times with his owner.

In order to continue participating in their owner's life after their initial assignment, a **God Animal will sometimes "over soul" other animals that reincarnate** to be with their original companion. Or they may

   Keep a watchful energy presence over its earthly person, or

   Be instrumental in instructing or assisting their earth person.

   Some God Animals meet and greet animals arriving after transition as Jiggs does for Lynn McKenzie.

©Peggy Iileen Johnson

Other God animals channel pertinent information to their humans, or organize and assist on a Universal plane with work that contributes to their human parent's efforts on earth like the wonderful stallion Lucero who is Ms. McKenzie's "other" partner.

© Brian Gibson

Some God Animals return to continue their mission on earth.

Can a pet return as a human?
• According to my experience and those of numerous renowned animal and interspecies communicators, pet psychics and intuitives, animals do not reincarnate in human form because an animal's body has a lower electromagnetic vibrational energy frequency than a human body.

Energy can easily reform at a like or lower level, but is not usually able to reincarnate into an energy frequency higher than the original spirit's frequency range.

On the other hand in the Yogic view, there are 8.4 million life times that souls evolve through, beginning with the lowest life forms.

In this Yogic belief system, it is understood that an animal can and will eventually evolve its vibration up to and become a human.

According to Yogic theory, sometimes an animal soul that becomes a human prematurely, before it has learned enough lessons to truly evolve, can reincarnate as a person that exhibits excessive "beast like" qualities.

In regards to the information in this entire book, always go with your inner guidance, and what resonates with you.

• **Animals that behave like humans**.
Human energy can adjust down into a lower frequency, so it is possible for a human to retain a pet body for a return incarnation.

However, more likely a human may "over soul" a pet. Usually older individuals that have transitioned will "over soul" a pet.

As an example, a friend had a dog that emulated all of the old characteristics of her husband who previously passed away. The husband's spirit was contributing his guidance and past knowledge to the current pet as an "over soul," (i.e. a soul in heaven who provides guidance and supervises over the earthly being). The "over soul" gives directives to the earth pet.

A pet being "over souled" will display more "acts like someone" traits rather than initiating within your heart that **deep** certain knowing that "it's my old pet reincarnated."

Is he "over souled" or reincarnated?

Sometimes even an owner can't tell which is which, but they WILL KNOW he's a "comeback."

Izzie's owner can't decide if he was a cat that now inhabits this dog body or is "over souled" by a strong feline presence.

Either way she **knows** they have been together in other lives.

Can my animal reincarnate into another pet form?

- Soul connected spirit guide and or guardian pets will select the most appropriate animal form to accompany you during the particular life phase that you will be sharing together.

- **Your pet may reincarnate either as a male or female or as a different breed of the same or another species.**

That lop-eared bunny love bug you had as a child may choose to return as your female "tigger kitty" then as a male Great Dane, and later as your horse when you're an adult.

Be open minded. Do not always expect the exact same physical image or gender.

- **More prevalent however is the fact that your pet will usually reincarnate within the same species** and within your animal preferences. After all, they know you well!

Animals will always have or exhibit special identifiable characteristics (that only you will know) in the early weeks of arrival in your life to insure you recognize them!

I prefer prick eared rough coated female red border collies. My "new" Friend is a male in his 5th reincarnation (with lots of female tendencies) prick eared medium coated tri color. Close enough! ☺- Especially with that bright white "B" on his bottom identical to my signature! Hello! I recognized him! ☺

Can my new puppy or a mature cat that was born BEFORE my pet died, be my reincarnated animal?

YES! At times your pet's new body will arrive on earth before your pet's old body passes away.

A "walk-in" is a pre arranged soul agreement (made in Heaven) between your original, to be deceased pet's spirit and the "delivery soul's" body.

After your original pet's spirit departs his old body, he then **"walks into" (i.e. transfer his soul's energy)** into the "new body" that was created and delivered to await his return.

When your pet enters the new vehicle, the "delivery soul" (like an auto company's driver delivering a new car) then returns to Heaven (the manufacturer), having completed his "delivery" job of transporting your pet's new body onto earth.

Sometimes the delivery body can arrive years in advance. That's why an older pet can become your "new" reincarnate.

The transfer of the contracting pet soul's energy "walking in" after its original body's death is still the same initial agreement. That new body just arrived earlier than expected, and the "delivery soul" had to wait around a little longer for the exchange to occur.

A "walk-in" transition process can occur immediately in a newborn, overnight or over a few months time. It is all determined by the animals' previous spiritual arrangement.

The best example of this "walk in" process is in the *"I'm Home!" a Dog's Never Ending Love Story* about Rinna and Darby and Austin's story in *"I'm Home!" a Dog's Never Ending Love Story.*

FYI, human "walk-ins" have many websites that can be found on the Internet that can further define and explain this process.

©Wayne Clarke

Can two pet souls occupy one body?
Yes. **A "soul braid"** occurs when a deceased pet's spirit blends with a current living pet's body and energy. The current pet then acts like and has characteristics of both animals.

A "soul braid," due to integration into and within a currently inhabited earth body takes a little more time and rearrangement of the two electromagnetics into one personality!

Oftentimes the living pet will appear to have a dehabilitating illness. That's when the process of electromagnetic interweaving of two soul frequencies into one body occurs.

When the living pet "gets well," it will display BOTH of the two pet's characteristics in the current earth body.   Miss Sisi (on the right below), later soul braided within Miss Angel (on the left) to stay with her beloved Victoria Ford longer.

In both the "walk-in" and "soul-braid" situation, your heart will understand, feel and inherently know what is transpiring as the new pet continues to display more and more special characteristics of your deceased pet or as in the case of the soul braid, BOTH pets!

How long does reincarnation take? What's the timing?

• There are times when your pet may have to attempt several different entrances BEFORE they get just the right body and circumstance to come back Home to you. Ollie's story in *"I'm Home!" a Cat's Never Ending Love Story* is a purrfect example ☺

• **Your pet's return can be as short as several hours or years later**. Be patient with whatever timeframe they require acquiring that new body, OR have prearranged to return to you.

• Be aware that sometimes your childhood pet doesn't't return until you are an adult. That's because your spiritual arrangement or each of your soul's contractual paths were for specific time periods in your life.

- To reiterate: It's possible that your old cat "walks in" to that new puppy or 3 month old stray or 9 year old rescue cat that has been "waiting" at the shelter in literally a heartbeat!

If your pet is a "walk-in", the "delivery" (body) can come in MANY forms and ages, because the "delivery" body was custom made for your pets "walk-in" return.
Age is not a factor.

Communicating with your pet on the other side:

Methods to communicate with your pet on the other side:

    Meditate and ask within your heart
    Use an animal or interspecies communicator,
        pet psychic, medium, intuitive or clairvoyant.
    Listen to your inner guidance and knowing
    Use the methods that resonate with you
        in any combination.

What can affect the communication with my pet on the other side?

The state of energy in which an animal passes affects the timeframe in which an animal communicator can contact your pet's energy.

Some very ill animals need to restore their original energy base before they are able to transmit information across the veils because they have a weak "signal." Other animals transmit from the other side loud and clear the minute they vacate the old body.

- If you are not comfortable with your inner guidance and or want further information to formulate your opinion, an animal or interspecies communicator, pet psychic, clairvoyant or spiritual medium often times can alert you to the fact that your pet will be or is returning and in what general form.

Some can also provide other information that might include the fact that your pet may already be here and waiting for you to find them!

Every gifted communicator will advise you to only use the information that resonates with your soul!

Signs your pet is contacting you from the other side

- On occasion your pet will leave little signs for you from the other side. You'll find toys in the floor that you thought you had previously stored. You'll hear noises of your other animals playing with the passed pet's spirit as an "imaginary friend."

- You can sense, see, smell, hear or feel your pet from the other side. You are <u>not</u> "crazy."

Many people feel their dogs and cats jump up on the bed each night as Mary would feel Rhett Butler do.

These pets do this so they can sleep with their person long after their old physical body has been discarded and up until they began the reentry process of reincarnation.

Many times I would hear Friend # 1 bark to protect me and make me aware of something, even when everything seemed very quiet.

I often saw Possum Kitty running from room to room and Hairy kitty darting playfully after dust bunnies, under my bed or into my open office drawer where she loved to sleep.

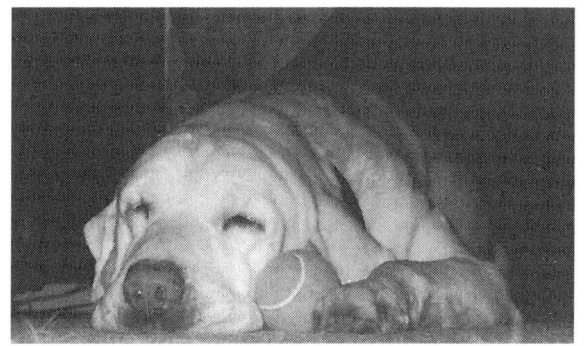

I see my yellow lab "Boo Bear" running across the golf course with his ball, so I know he's happy.

Oftentimes your pet will superimpose their old visual physical image over the new reincarnate's body to insure that you understand and know "it's me again!" Union Jack's Story in *"I'm Home!" a Dog's Never Ending Love Story* is a wonderful example.

I can still feel Electra my "squirrel girl" close to my side when I am extremely upset or afraid and during summer "boomies" (thunderstorms).

Your pet's signs will be very clear distinct, yet random or ongoing incidents and feelings that your heart and soul WILL recognize and KNOW it's them!

- Your pet will visit in your dreams.

- When you are crying nonstop, praying or just wondering if your beloved four legged family member is okay, sometimes your pet will cause a commotion or distraction that you **know in your heart** is their response to let you know that they are just fine.

A friend's deceased dog Revel would use his energy to knock his pictures off her table when she was upset, to let her know that he was still watching over her from the other side.

© Diane Lewis Photography

When your crying and anger subsides, **you will have greater clarity about the reincarnation process and all its subliminal signs and nuances** that you may have missed while being so upset.

How To Contact Your Pet's Energy and Bring It Into Earth Energy:
State:
I ask and it is my intent
to contact the energy previously known as

_____,
so that I can feel him now.
I ask _____ to put your paw (nose, head, whatever)
into my _____hand now.

I say this prayer 3 times to create focus. Use these exact words. They protect you and they produce, in time, positive results!

Sometimes it takes up to 2 weeks until your pet will respond. Various research materials suggest that you should ask to "contact" your pet (this works with people too!) at the same time each day for quicker results. You can also set your intent and ask to see and communicate with a pet in your dreams.

How to Find and Touch Your Pet's Energy Across the Veils:

My deceased fiancé taught me how to do this. Before he died, I did not know this was even possible! After I learned this process, we would hold hands when I was afraid, and he would kiss me every night before I went to sleep. I learned that energy and love is infinite!

When your pet has responded to your prayer to be present in earth energy you'll sense them. Now it's time to "feel" their energy.

1. Rub your hands together until they are warm in order to activate the nerve endings in your palms and fingertips so you can sense energy to the "max."

2. Then spread your fingers apart with about -at least- a half inch of space between each finger like a wide toothed comb.

3. Softly as if you are trying to touch the dust on butterfly wings, sweep your hands horizontally back and forth within about a 4 foot wide path about 4 feet high rectangular area in the vicinity you are sense your pet is located.

You scan for their energy by taking your hand palm open fingers like a comb and carefully and very slowly sweeping back and forth left to right or vice versa and top to bottom through the space you sense they may be in.

Keep working in rectangular quadrants until you feel and sense a thicker, denser, usually cooler mass within the target area. That's them! You can feel the edges of their form, even all their "feetsies" or feathers! If you get REALLY good, you can feel their whiskers.

This may take some time; your reward is worth it!

"Getting sensitive to a different feel of air" is how you will learn. Don't get frustrated, in time it works.

The softer, more consistent your movements are and the slower (i.e. don't rush this) you approach any energy field, the greater the sensory input you will receive.

Your transitioned animal's energy field will feel thicker than normal air, tingly or cold. Your heart will KNOW it's them! Be patient and practice, practice, practice! This will allow tangible recognition to occur more rapidly.

One of my clients would get her cat to lie around her shoulders. She also would have him put his paw in her hand on command. You can even feel your animal kiss you! Or bump into you with that ball you should be throwing.

This may take some getting used to, but it's worth every minute spent!

Why is this exercise so informative?

Once you have learned to feel, connect and resonate with your pet's energy across the veils, your soul will be more "in tune" to and resonate with what they "feel like."

This knowing will allow you to be more sensitive to their reincarnation progress. You will be able to inwardly "feel" them getting closer, like waves of energy building more and more as they come closer into the earth energy.

When their new earth body arrives, your heart will "beam them up" and there is NO way you will misinterpret your intuitive inner directives and urgings of finding them, and knowing where they are. You will just "feel it!"

You're probably wondering:

1. Now that my pet's energy is visiting me, what do I do with it?
   Enjoy your new awareness and your pet!

2. If I contact my animal's spirit, am I interrupting his/her spirit from whatever it is supposed to be doing on the other side? NO!

Is contacting my pet's energy selfish?

When you are each other's "true love," then keeping in touch is not a burden. However, it IS your pet's choice to respond to your invitation for a visit.

Sometimes an animal will just "show up" on their own accord. Your desire to have **obsessive** contact can be bad for your animal's spiritual energy and its long-term transition to a higher realm or back to you.

When your pet no longer wants to respond or has moved to a higher plane, then you will be unable to do this form of contact.

Example, Mike my fiancé who was killed, came to visit me on multiple occasions including my birthday and our anniversaries. However after several years he no longer appeared. I inherently knew that he had moved forward into another realm.

What can prohibit my pet from visiting me?
Sometimes your grief prohibits their spirit's ability to contact you and come into your consciousness.

You have to be open minded for this to occur and your energy accepting of their arrival.

Example, after Mike was killed, he would begin to formulate in spirit form in front of me. I was so scared that I would not allow him to do that! I was so emotionally upset that I couldn't handle it!

It is my greatest regret that I did not allow Mike to present himself as a living energy to me, when he was in the energy state of being able to assemble into a recognizable form.

Many individuals have had their beloved deceased people or pets visit and it was very comforting and healing. There is nothing to fear.

FYI, I'm using my human experiences with my fiancé as the foundation of how I know this is possible. The process of communication in this manner is the same either with a human or animal.

The stages of your animal's return
Grieving:

- Initially you really miss your pet more than a mere animal loss. You recognize he had a "special bond" with you and that you were blessed to share life with him. You feel "we aren't done yet."

Feeling that "special bond," "blessed" and "aren't through" is your soul's recognition and understanding that your pet has a shared soul growth involvement with you in this lifetime. You have things to learn "together."

- At times you may be angry due to the manner in which your pet died. The sooner you release your anger, the more receptive you are to receiving your new buddy.

Your anger and grief over your animal's death blocks and stalls any of your pet's contact or energy movement back into your life- dreams, visits and reincarnation.

As soon as you can, celebrate the fact that your beloved companion is on the way back home. He/she just has to get a replacement body to keep on "keeping on" with you!

- During bereavement, if you still feel that you want to hold onto your pet's beds, bowl and toys, collar, et al, usually there is a deeper reason.

Your inner guidance inherently knows that they will be back.

Just keep his/her possessions in a safe place to let him know you understand he'll return and is not forgotten.

Your pet is reminding you they are OK or that their return is drawing closer when you are:

"Seeing" their energy out of the corner of your eye, seeing them in recurrent dreams.

"Feeling" their presence like lying in your lap, jumping on the bed or leaving toys out.

"Hearing" them doing something familiar (licking fur, playing with one of your current live pets)

Experiencing other little "announcements" that YOU understand!

***** You are not going crazy! *****

Do those signs mean there are definitely returning?

If reincarnating, your pet will provide even more and more obvious and frequent notice that their spirit's energy is adapting back into the earth's energy and they are on the way!

Then, as an animal seriously approaches reentry for reincarnation, these experiences will stop as they refocus all of their energy into reassembling for their return!

At that point in time, you will already know in your soul from all of the confirmations you have previously received, that cessation of these contact signs does NOT mean they are not returning.

If your pet **is NOT reincarnating** it's their way of visiting you and checking in.

How can you tell the difference?

It's not easy. Using the prayers to ask your pet directly helps your clarity.

When your prayers are answered with a "no," and these incidents become more and more sporadic like a personal "call" from a long time friend over the ongoing years, your heart will know and understand that your pet is just checking in on you and is not going to return.

Brent Atwater's
Just Plain Love® Books presents

Reconnection:
How will we get back together?

- Listen to and trust when and where your intuition and inner guidance leads you to initiate your reconnection.

Act immediately! Do not delay the timing and guidance of your inner urgings when your heart compels or incessantly nags you to search for your pet's new body form.

- You will instinctively be led to, and will "know" whether to look for a puppy, a rescue animal, in an animal shelter, on an internet search or in a newspaper ad.

Your pet may just wander up and appear out of "nowhere." Someone may call you to "come see" this wonderful fur, finned or feathered creature that they have found or was "just turned in." GO! Have you left yet?

- If you are new to listening to your inner guidance, let's say this again: Never overlook the little details and just pass them off as not worthy of attention.

Follow through on all information presented to you, **at the time it is presented** and trust it is correct. All the myriad domino effects lead to your pet! **There are no coincidences!**

- Do NOT be discouraged by "he's already taken or been adopted," or sold or not available. If you KNOW in your heart that this is

YOUR pet, be steadfast, keep going forward and do not be discouraged or deterred by what you perceive as current roadblocks. Kim and Sidey's adventure in *"I'm Home!" a Dog's Never Ending Love Story* is a great example of this principle.

© Diane Lewis Photography

When it's your animal companion, all things will just "work out" in some of the most interesting, amazing and <u>*unbelievable*</u> ways for you to be together again!

An "adopted" pet may never get picked up, a deposit never honored, people change their minds! The Universe will see that you are reunited one way or another!
YOU can't mess it up!

- If you don't have that "certain knowing" in your heart and the details don't work out for you to get a particular animal, that's the Universe letting you know, it's not the right one! It's NOT your reincarnated pet!

The Universe actually helps steer you by making SURE that you don't get the wrong pet! When it's the correct reincarnate, the Universe will arrange to make all things possible to bring your companion home!

Recognition:
How will I recognize MY pet?
- Do NOT allow anyone who is outside your heartfelt circle tell you it's your pet reincarnated!!!

ONLY you and those very close to your pet's soul when he/she was alive will actually feel and know that true soul recognition!

Remember this in your loneliest moments so you don't get caught up in other people's opinions or swayed by paid advisors:

ONLY your soul integrated with your pet's energy vibration, you and he are "One."

Only YOU will TRULY recognize his/her presence as a new incarnate or his guidance to your new pet.

I could FEEL Friend in my heart!
I actually missed the "B" on his hip because I was so caught up in and overwhelmed by my emotions!

My close friends, who were an integral part of my previous reincarnates lives, immediately recognized when they saw the video, that it was MY Friend returning home to me!

They pointed out that the "B" in Friend's fur looked like my signature, and that God obviously knew I needed "confirmation."

- **A visual soul recognition story**:

One Saturday afternoon, a lady felt strong inner urges to drive to a shelter to find a dog to fill her heart's void until (she thought) her beloved pet reincarnated.

When she and her husband pulled into the parking lot, her soul recognition kicked in.

There, walking across the parking lot toward the shelter was her reincarnated pet on a leash with someone else!

Coincidentally, the Universe had prearranged for another family to take her reincarnated puppy to the shelter at that very moment. They were turning the puppy in for adoption.

Timing is everything!
She immediately adopted HER dog!

- **Your pet will also choose you** in order to assist you in recognizing their reincarnated form!

They will choose you under any and all circumstances. They know you, and there is no doubt about it when they pick you! This fact applies even if they are living with another individual before coming back into your life.

Judy visited her cousin and was adopted immediately by her cousin's "Westie." After Judy left, that dog mourned, whined, would not eat, etc, so much that Judy's cousin finally gave her the Westie for the "dog's sake."

Loui was happily reunited with "her person" Judy for 17 more years.

Could I miss my pet and the "signs?"

Absolutely not!
The Universe will insure that you do not make the wrong choice by intervening and will insure that you make the correct choice with perfect coincidences.
Your heart will "know that feeling" when you connect!

As your pet gets closer and closer, their

approaching energy will produce more and more waves of compelling intuitive guidance.

Like pre birth contractions, the waves of energy as your pet re-enters the earth dimension will be felt as Inner guidance "contractions" with increasing frequency to inspire and push you to look for them. These "nudgies" propel you until you DO reunite with them or they find you!

Can my deceased pet's spirit, lead me to their new earth body?
Absolutely! Just follow your inner urgings!

Confirmation:
- Look into your pet's eyes, the windows of their soul. Your heart will **know** them and **feel** the connection you share and have shared. It's **soul recognition**!

- Ask your pet questions with your soul and listen to their answers with your heart.

- **Your pet will bond with you right away, almost immediately**!

Even if they are a "walk-in "or "soul braid" as illustrated in the *"I'm Home!"* Books' stories, you will still KNOW it's your pet as they make their spirit's transition into their new body!

- **Reincarnates respond immediately to all the old "things."**

Often times your new pet even responds to your old pet's name and knows exactly where all the old pet's possessions are located.

Sometimes they recognize their old home! In one of the stories in *"I'm Home!" a Dog's Never Ending Love Story* (see Union Jack's story), a young pup recognized his old home and tried to get out of the car while riding past it on the way to his person's new house!

- **Their emotional behavior traits, quirky loveable habits and physical mannerisms are uncannily similar,** right down to sleeping in the same location in "that funny position," turning their head a certain way, liking the exact food (like eating ice cubes), and even disliking or liking the same pet in your current household, etc.

- Your "new" reincarnated animal (puppy, kitten, bunny, ferret, bird, foal, or Beta Fish, etc) **will act like an adult much sooner** than expected and will display fewer "new baby" behaviors and attitudes.

- A "walk in" or "over-soul" pet's traits will be uncannily the same or VERY similar from the get go. You'll have very few doubts that's it's your returned forever buddy!

- **Current household animals that lived with the transitioned pet will recognize the "new" old soul.**

The reincarnates also will have some of the same grudges and disputes with the same animals.

My dog Friend always got along with our cat Mikey; however he never liked "Ugly, the most beautiful cat of them all." They still don't get along. I had hoped Heaven would have expanded his patience!

Brent Atwater's
Just Plain Love® Books presents

- Oftentimes when your pet comes back, they will embody a new trait that you had been hoping they would have. These new traits may also contribute to your future path together.

My previous "Sunday dogs" were never "child friendly" because they lived with a single adult and were never exposed to children.

New Friend is a child/ people magnet. He thinks he's "human." The Universe obviously knew that this will be a wonderful trait for his paw/book signings, guest appearances for fundraising and pet therapy work with children and visitations in health care facilities!

Reuniting: "I'm Home!"

No matter where your pet's energy is, whether they reincarnate or not, your beloved finned, furry or feathered
soul connected companion will always be a part of your heart forever and always!!!

Because
Love is never ending!

The Animal Reincarnation Guide:
Everything You Always Wanted to Know!

In your darkest hours after transition,
Choose hope!
Your pet might be just a heartbeat away!

Soon you'll feel
"I'm Home!"

Animal Reincarnation is REAL!!!
Just ask *Friend*

the Dog with **my** "B" on His Bottom!

Brent Atwater's
Just Plain Love® Books presents

Are there any More Questions from the Audience?

Why are some animal communicators unable to determine if my pet is going to return?

A person who reads "energy," whether it's a psychic, intuitive or animal/ interspecies communicator can only "tune into" the band width frequency that they are able to and capable of "reading or receiving."

Think of it this way, when you tune a radio to a specific frequency, you get a specific station.

Each communicator or intuitive has a specific frequency bandwidth that they receive information from. If your reader is unable to tune in to 100 am i.e. Fluffy's station, then they do not get the same information as another communicator who CAN tap into bandwidth 100 am.

No reading is less or more importance than another. Each reader can tap into a specific energy frequency bandwidth. The range of a readers' bandwidth is what determines how much a reader is able to "tap into" from your pet's individual energy imprint.

It's the same with humans. Some readers you think are great, because the "get" your station. Others cannot provide a good reading for you simply because they do not have the ability to tune into your station's frequency!

Why do different animal communicators give me different and conflicting information and details or provide varying timeframes about my pet's return?

As stated above, each reader has the ability to pick up on certain information from the channels that are available to them. Readings vary because you are getting information from each of the different "stations and channels!"

If you get two intuitives on the same station, the information will be very similar.

What is the difference between Human energy and Animal energy?

Every living being has an electromagnetic vibrational frequency. That frequency determines their individual electromagnetic imprint or identity.

Human energy has a range of 68- 72 MHz as a healthy human frequency. FYI, even each organ in your body had a specific vibrational frequency identity. Vibrational medicine addresses these frequencies in resolving health issues, and there is lots of wonderful information on the internet.

Animal Energy frequencies vibrate at a lower MHz level than human energy.

What happens to animals left in shelters, do they reincarnate?

Location does not determine or effect any previous spiritual arrangements. Any animal anywhere can create a soul's contract to reincarnate if it's their choice and part of their soul's path.

Do service/guide dogs reincarnate?
That is each individual animal's choice. Please read the God Animal section for further clarification and see Austin's story in *"I'm Home!" a Dog's Never Ending Love Story.*

Do animals have a spiritual awareness?
In my opinion, the very fact that pets DO reincarnate indicates a spiritual awareness of the soul arrangement made with their human guardian.

Animals survive on their instincts which are highly evolved senses and intuition that make up their level of consciousness. They operate completely in the present.

Animals act from their wholeness, and comprehend beyond the bounds of known reality.

Many owners and pets read each other's mind and communicate telepathically which is considered a "spiritual" awareness and interchange. Some can sense unseen "energy" intrusions like the Seizure dogs.

Do animals have reincarnation choices like a human?
Yes.
Its their choice to return or not, and to honor a spiritual arrangement with you.

Do cats and dogs tutor others?
Yes.

That's what we call an "over-soul," where the deceased pet directs the living pet on "what to do" and "how to behave" from Heaven.

Secondly, the God Animals, direct the lives of live animals. Note the previous example of Jiggs the Golden Retriever who assists animals during transition and after they have crossed the Rainbow Bridge.

Do pets reincarnate for the greater good of other pets?
Yes. As examples:

The animals that you find homeless in shelters, that are euthanized, living in horrific and other heinous conditions have volunteered their lives to help change the conditions for the greater good of other animals.

The horses in Central Park that became overexerted in the midday heat changed the conditions for other equines. New laws were passed to correct those conditions.

The dolphins that were caught in fishing nets or beached whales led the way to reform and solutions that bettered the lives for all those animals that followed.

Do pets on the other side interact with animals on earth since they interact with humans?
Yes.

Because animals live by their keen instincts, they are very aware of energies and entities from across the veils. Often times your earth pet will continue to "play" or interact with the deceased animal's living energy.

They may growl over the food bowl at an imaginary friend, or bat a paw at a plain air playmate. There have been times when, as an example, a living horse would neigh, paw and nod when his deceased equine companion would visit the barn.

Does the behavior of live pets playing with deceased animals predict the fact that the deceased pet is going to reincarnate?
No.
It's just a sign that animals are very aware of "all there is."

And last but not least…..
If I freeze my pet's body after transition for the taxidermist, will it affect their reincarnation?
No!
However, you need to get the old body to the taxidermist as soon as possible so bacteria will not destroy the tissue or infect your freezer.

In the beautiful full color *"I'm Home!"* books meet some of the people and their animal companions and pets that provided the foundational evidence for my research and that exemplify the various concepts of the reincarnation process.

"I'm Home!" a Dog's Never Ending Love Story

"I'm Home!" a Cat's Never Ending Love Story

"I'm Home!" a Horse's Never Ending Love Story

Message to Book Clubs and Professional Associations and Organizations

I'd be delighted to speak with you over the phone or schedule a presentation.

Please email me at
Brent@BrentAtwater.com

BrentAtwater@live.com

Brent's motto:
"I want my books and art to DO good,
as well as BE good!"

Brent Atwater and "Friend" (who's on his 5th reincarnation with a "B" on his Bottom) are pet reincarnation authorities who travel the world educating and expanding awareness about animal reincarnation and answered prayers!

Brent has devoted decades of research to pet reincarnation and her findings are a treasure! There are not enough books like this one examining the never ending bond, spiritual arrangements and healing between you and your pet. These stores are a celebration of love at its best!

As a medical intuitive, Brent can see the organs, nerves, bones, tissue et al inside your body, diagnose and also predict future physical energy events. Therefore Ms Atwater can determine if and when your pet is going to reincarnate.

In order to talk with your pet, contact your favorite animal or interspecies communicator.

Brent Atwater helps change lives in addition to inspiring hope by providing you and your pet tools, techniques and solutions that enable you and your animal companions to communicate, facilitate healing and to have a better quality of life.

Ms. Atwater's leading edge medical intuitive work, energy healing and educational consultations have assisted countless individuals and their cherished pets.

Brent Atwater pioneered and founded the field of medical intuitive diagnostic imaging™ (MIDI) for humans and, AMIDI for animals. Her work with a global clientele has documented, published and respected case results. She collaborates with and participates in ongoing energy medicine, medical intuitive diagnostic research and independent case and pilot studies with the world are leading investigators.

Ms. Atwater's work establishes evidence based research that creates and documents the bridging of traditional medicine with alternative therapies into holistic integrative medicine.

Ms Atwater is also a pioneer in healing art

medicine by scientifically documenting the healing energy, diagnostic abilities and healing benefits of her art for healthcare Paintings *That Heal*® (www.BrentAtwater.com). She is one of the contemporary American painters who are bringing forth a new cultural renaissance by blending her classical artistic training with spirituality and energy infused into her healing art.

Brent Atwater's *Just Plain Love*® *Books,* weekly radio shows, podcasts, blogs, invigorating and inspiring audience participatory workshops (with awesome demonstrations), upbeat seminars, speaking tours, presentations and consultations bring about transformative and positive results.

And book signings with her pet therapy dog Friend are more than fun!

The Just Plain Love® Story

"Experiencing a pediatric intensive care, oncology, burn or trauma unit to me, is a heart wrenching jolt to anyone's world. I had to summon all my "heart" to handle the various states of disrupted life. Right then and there I decided that a positive Light needed to shine on the hearts and minds of these struggling little souls, so new to earth and so old to the diseases, health issues and medical conditions whose very procedures and treatments ravaged their young bodies.

I decided that I was going to find a way to offer a "positive spin" on all of the health issue negatives and to create a portal of communication, and a treasure of heartwarming and reassuring perspectives to those "hands off" subjects.

Additionally I want to inspire a muffled laugh, instigate a tiny smile, mischievous giggle or just create an environmental change and safe place for even a brief moment that would add a sparkle to a weary eye.

AND I was going to give a comforting and supportive symbolic "hug" to each patient and reader by filling them with a sense of pride in themselves for having endured their own health battle and surrounding issues. Plus, I would provide a tangible and permanent way to honor and celebrate their courage!

I was unable to have children, so this is my way of giving back.
In 1987 the Just Plain Love® Charitable Trust was born."

Brent Atwater's Other Dream:
Just Plain Love® Plays, Performances & Educational Programs for Children with "Poof" the Angel & "Friend" the pet angel therapy dog.

Surely, Ms Atwater dreams, there can be participatory mini skits/plays held in healthcare and medical facilities lasting about 5 to 15 minutes that would hold a patient's attention, entertain, educate, rehabilitate and provide a few safe moments of mental relief through laughter, plus providing each patient with a tangible Badge of Honor to reward and recognize their courage.

For the past 20+ years Brent Atwater has researched, tested, rewritten and reworked each children's healing book and play according to the storytelling responses and reactions from healthy and unhealthy readers, caregivers, family, friends, medical and healthcare professionals, clients and her storytelling audience.

Brent Atwater's dream is to inspire the creative imagination of readers of all ages to replace negative thoughts about health issues, medical experiences, rehabilitative therapy and reentry into society with a positive "spin" on their journey to health and well being.

Visit
www.BrentAtwater.com
www.JustPlainLoveBooks.com

Follow Brent on
Twitter, Tumbler, Facebook, YouTube, MySpace et al.

Be sure to read our other full color wonderful Just Plain Love® animal reincarnation stories

"I'm Home!" a Dog's Never Ending Love Story
"I'm Home!" a Cat's Never Ending Love Story
"I'm Home!" a Horse's Never Ending Love Story

We invite you to submit your story for future books!

Friend is available for paw signings guest appearances, fundraising & hugs!

As are some of the other wonderful reincarnated pets that have shared their stories with in our books!

Contact: Brent Atwater

Join Friend's
MySpace and Facebook groups for more pet reincarnation stories and to share yours!

http://groups.myspace.com/petreincarnation
http://www.facebook.com/group.php?gid=59877299590

Become a fan of Friend Atwater's Official Facebook Site for
"I'm Home!" a Dog's Never Ending Love Story

**Visit Friend's
Facebook , Twitter , YouTube, Tumblr and MySpace**

Subscribe to our Blogs

Just Plain Love® Books

inspiring thoughts that provide smiles, hugs and healing for every reader's heart!

Other Just Plain Love® Titles
in Audio, EBooks, Hardcover, Kindle, and Paperback

Children's Books:
Cancer Kids—God's Special Children!
Cancer and MY Daddy

Holistic Integrative Energy Medicine, Intuitive Development:
Medical Intuition, Intuitive Diagnosis,
Medical Intuitive Diagnostic Imaging™ (MIDI) &
Animal Medical Intuitive Diagnostic Imaging™

The Encyclopedia of Bioenergy Patterns that
Identify & Diagnose Diseases & Disorders
Animal Intuitive Diagnosis AMIDI

Self Help Healing, Mind Body Connection:
Healing Yourself! 23 Ways to Heal Diseases and Disorders

Animal Lovers' Books:
the Dog with a "B" on His Bottom!
"I'm Home!" a Dog's Never Ending Love Story
Pet Reincarnation & Animal Communication
"I'm Home!" a Cat's Never Ending Love Story
"I'm Home!" a Horse's Never Ending Love Story
Animal Reincarnation Guide:
Everything You Always Wanted to Know!

We hope you enjoyed our
Just Plain Love® Book.

Want more information about *Just Plain Love® Books*,
contact: Brent@BrentAtwater.com

Visit Brent Atwater's websites:
www.BrentAtwater.com
www.JustPlainLoveBooks.com
www.BrentEnergyWork.com

This material is internationally copyrighted with all rights reserved to
B. Brent Atwater. None of this material may be used or reproduced without written permission of B. Brent Atwater.
Animal Reincarnation Guide:
Everything You Always Wanted to Know!
© 2008-2011

Made in the USA
Lexington, KY
10 February 2011